The Sunday Ladle

Hungary to Cuba to America:
A Love Story With Recipes

by

Olga Weiss Hipschman

International Standard Book Number 13: 978-1-60452-113-9
International Standard Book Number 10: 1-60452-113-9
Library of Congress Control Number: 2016903004

BluewaterPress LLC
52 Tuscan Way Ste 202-309
Saint Augustine FL 32092
www.bluewaterpress.com

This book may be purchased online at -

www.bluewaterpress.com/ladle

Please note that address information is subject to change. At the time of printing, the address was correct, but may have changed since. Please check our website for the latest address information for BluewaterPress LLC.

Acknowledgments

Cover design by Katie Hipschman

Cover photo used by permission courtesy of
Dr. Anne Brown and www.scottishpottery.weebly.com

The author gratefully acknowledges the work of her editor,
David Hipschman

Dedication

To my dear husband, whose love and encouragement helped me to pursue my dreams. To my four children, who are the blessings of my life, and to my dear grandchildren, who give me reason to keep hoping for the future.

Author's Note

This is a memoir of events, many of which took place in the author's childhood. Memory is inexact; any errors are the author's and unintended.

A Note on the Recipes

Cooking, the way I learned in my mother's kitchen, was done with measurement like "a pinch," or "salt to taste." I have over the years translated such into teaspoons, tablespoons and the like. But remember that a recipe is only a guide; trust your own taste buds!

There is a mixture called "Mom's Spice" referred to in some of the recipes, if you choose to use it, remember to eliminate any salt and pepper from the list of ingredients.

Mom's Spice is the following mixed together and kept in a jar for frequent use: 2 tsp. of garlic powder, 1 tsp. of lemon pepper, 1 tsp. of oregano, 1 tsp. of sweet paprika, 1 tsp. of onion powder, 1 tsp., of chili powder and 1 tsp. of salt.

Contents

Chapter 1

Maria

Maria wasn't sure what she was going to do with the day.

It was Friday and her two older brothers had left early to travel to Bucharest, across the border in Romania, to find work. Her father had gone to the neighbor's vineyards, three miles away, to tend to their grapevines. It was early spring and he was always called to tie the vines of the Tokay grapes and prune them to see if there was any winter damage. Andras was considered the best wine maker in the region. He loved his work and talked to the vines and sung to them as though they were his children.

Her mother Teresa was in the kitchen preparing the winter cabbage for the strudel filling and the cabbage noodles they would be having for their main meal later that day. The large iron stove was already warming up the entire kitchen. Her brothers had filled it with wood and lit it before they left.

* * *

Teresa would place the flour and the eggs on the wooden table she had next to the large stove and deftly began to knead the dough until it was ready. She would cut then roll each section thinly and spread each thin round on the back of the wooden chairs to dry. When dried, she would roll each section of dough to cut in different sizes and shapes. Left in their own mounds to dry, they then would be wrapped in linen cloths and placed in the pantry on shelves to dry further.

* * *

Cabbage Noodles

1 small cabbage shredded
4 tbsp. butter melted in skillet
1tsp sugar

Sauté:
Sauté until golden. Add salt and pepper to taste stirring often.

Simmer:
Cover and simmer on low heat.

Homemade Noodles

2 cups all purpose flour, sifted
4 to 5 tbsp. water
2 eggs
1 tsp. salt

Mix and knead:

Place flour in a bowl. Make a well. Add remaining ingredients. Mix and knead well until dough comes together and is shiny. Cover with a cloth and let rest a few minutes.

Roll, Cut, Boil:

Roll dough on floured board until very thin and allow to dry about an hour. Cut in shapes desired before boiling in salted water. They are done when they rise to the surface, about 2 minutes. Drain well and mix with the sautéed cabbage. Correct seasonings.

* * *

Usually, Maria would help her mother in the kitchen. Her younger sister and brother would always follow her around, trying to help her but only getting in the way. They loved Maria, especially when she would sing the lovely Hungarian songs for them as she helped set the table. On this morning, as she went out toward the well through their small kitchen garden, she saw someone approach in the distance. As he neared, she noted it was a young man of perhaps 20 or 21 years of age, riding a Bay horse. The young man was dressed all in black, had dark curly black hair and soft brown eyes. As he got closer, she noted a warm smile on his face. Her heart skipped as he stopped and quickly dismounted.

"Hello, may I have some water for my horse?" and smiling, while looking deep into her eyes, asked "and for myself?"

Blushing, Maria answered, "Of course, but just a moment."

She turned and ran towards the house shouting, "Mama, Mama, there's a man here asking for water and I'm getting the Sunday ladle for him to drink from."

Maria ran towards the dining room and removed the ladle, which hung on the wall. The ladle was used on Sundays and for special guests. It had beautiful flowers painted on the porcelain dipper.

She ran back to the well. The young man had drawn water for his horse with the pail. Maria drew water with another pail, dipped the ladle in the cool clear water and handed it to him to drink from.

The young man said, "My name is Nicolas, what is yours?"

Lowering her head, she answered him.

He smiled as she came towards his horse, patted his head and asked, "What is his name?"

"Gypsy" answered Nicolas, "I've raised him from a colt and he is my favorite companion."

They looked at each other, Maria with her long wavy chestnut-colored hair and hazel eyes with the golden sparkles, and Nicolas who had never felt like this before.

He knew he had to hurry and leave. Today, his family prepared for the Sabbath and his father would be waiting for him to help collect the rent from the sharecroppers who tilled the soil to grow their produce. Nicolas knew he should not be where he was. He had wandered too far from home.

Nicolas

Lately, he had felt stifled at home. He loved his parents and his brothers and sisters and especially the Sabbath preparations.

The entire house was scrubbed shiny clean. The smells of cooking and baking filled the air. His mother and sisters and the maids would cook and bake the meals for two full days for the entire family as well as the company of rabbinical students his father would bring home from the synagogue after the services. These were students studying to become rabbis, most of them poor, who looked forward to the Sabbath meals at the Weiss' home. His father was the president of the synagogue and was very involved in the community.

Nicolas' grandfather had been a scribe, a sofer. He remembered when he was a child they went to visit him. His grandfather would be in a small room, hunched over a tilted table that was covered with a white linen cloth. On top of the table there would lay a scroll of parchment. He would dip his pen in black ink and slowly and methodically would etch a Hebrew word on the parchment, from right to left. He would wash his hands, dry them with a white linen cloth and then say a prayer. He would do that with each word he printed.

Nicolas always enjoyed the Sabbath meal best. The Friday night meal was served after the Sabbath candles were lit and after the blessing over the Challah. This Golden Chicken soup was his favorite.

* * *

Golden Chicken Soup

1 whole large hen (5-6 lbs.)
3 stalks celery
8 peppercorns*
4 quarts water
3 large carrots, peeled
1 tomato
1 tbsp. salt
1/2 tsp. pepper
1 large onion with skin
½ green pepper
Parsnip
Parsley

*The reason the peppercorns were counted was to account for them after the soup was strained so that no one would bite into one.

Boil and Simmer:
Place chicken in enough cold water to cover it in a large pot. Bring to a boil, then simmer slowly for about 2 hours. Add rest of ingredients and simmer an extra hour or so. Skim off top of soup a few times while cooking. When done, remove

vegetables and place on a platter. Leave whole chicken in broth until cool. Correct the seasoning and skim off fat from top of broth. Drain chicken and place on platter, cut in pieces. Lay the root vegetables around the chicken.

Place cheesecloth on large strainer and place strainer in another large pot. Strain broth. Chicken can be used as part of a main dish or for chicken salad the next day.

* * *

Matzo Balls

2 eggs
1 tbsp. fat from top of soup
1 tsp. salt
½ tsp. pepper
1/8 cup chicken broth (as needed)
1 tsp. chopped dill or parsley
1 tsp. baking soda

Mix together:
Mix all ingredients. Then add ¾ to 1 cup matzo meal
Refrigerate 20 minutes.

Boil:
Bring 4 quarts salted water to boil. Place sprig of dill or parsley in water. Use a tablespoon to make rounded matzo balls. Wet palm of hand and form balls. Drop in boiling water and cover. Simmer gently till done. (About 20 minutes).

* * *

Stuffed Roasted Broilers

Three 2- 2 ½ lb. chickens

Dry rub:
Rub with salt, white pepper, sweet paprika, and vegetable oil inside and out.

Roast in Oven
Roast 1½ hrs. at 350 degrees, turning every 20 minutes. You may stuff under the skin.

* * *

Stuffing

2 chicken livers, chopped
1 onion chopped
1diced garlic clove
3 eggs
1 tsp. salt and ¼ tsp. white pepper,
or use Mom's Spice
3 tbsp. vegetable oil
Parsley, chopped
6 thick slices dry egg bread (Challah) soaked in broth
4 chopped mushrooms

Soak bread:
Soak bread in chicken broth.

Sauté:
Sauté onion, mushrooms and chicken livers in the oil until golden.

Stuff:

Squeeze bread and chop fine and mix all ingredients and gently stuff chickens under the skin lifting skin with fingers and tie legs together with string. Rub seasonings all over chicken.

Roast:
Place oiled chickens in heavy baking pan and roast for about 1½ hours to 2 hours turning every 20 minutes till roasted crisp. Be careful not to pierce skin.

Allow to cool and cut into quarters and serve on a large platter.

* * *

Sabbath Meal

Everyone looked forward to the Cholent, a cassoulet of beans, barley and fatty fowl or meats baked in an oven for 24 hours. It was served during the Sabbath when there was no cooking done.

It was Nicolas' job to place the large heavy kettle on a small wagon, hook Gypsy to it and take it to the town baker's oven. Along with the rest of the townspeople, the kettles would be placed in the baker's large brick oven to bake slowly for 24 hours. Somehow, everyone knew their own pot!

* * *

Cholent (Casoulette)

1 chopped onion
1 lb. small white beans
½ lb. barley
1 large fowl with fat or ½ goose and ½ fowl.
1 tbsp. salt
½ tsp. pepper
2 crushed garlic cloves

1 tbsp. sweet paprika
Chicken broth to cover all

Boil, then Bake:
Bring to a boil, place in a 300 ° oven and bake overnight.
Add water if needed. Mix and uncover last hour to form a crust on top at 350° sprinkling some paprika twice over all and mix.

* * *

But lately, Nicolas felt as though he wanted to travel and find a new life in another part of the world, perhaps America. He heard there were many opportunities there and he felt as though he was ready to go.

The Great War had ended and many of his countrymen had come back and many did not. His father had served in the Hungarian Army and when he returned he had many ideas to improve the land they lived on. Times were changing and he had read of new technology to increase production of his crops. The land had been handed down to him by his father and grandfather. When there was an opportunity he would buy more land. He had three sons who would carry on. He relied on Nicolas to collect the rents from the sharecroppers who tilled and sowed the fields for their own use, and in return would give a percentage of the yield to the Weiss family.

The fields would be filled with the beautiful golden sunflowers, row after row, each heavy with their seed pods, which, when dry in the fall, would be cut and gathered and processed into oil. Some of the oil was kept for family use, some sold in the market for the townspeople and the balance sold to the traders and taken to markets in nearby towns

Nicolas jumped back on his horse, and said "Farewell, beautiful Maria. Maybe we'll meet again someday." And off he rode at a fast canter.

Maria stood and watched him leave until she could not see him anymore. She felt a strange sadness overcome her and turned back to the house. She stopped, turned toward the road, and thought of the young stranger. Who was he? Where did he come from? The funny longing returned. "I wish I knew," she sighed.

She hung the ladle back on its hook on the dining room wall.

"Mari what are you dreaming of? Come set the table, your father will be home soon for dinner," her mother said.

The family would have a big meal at midday and supper was leftovers. The wonderful deep scent of the bacon and chicken in the sauce permeated the entire house. She placed the pieces of chicken on a large platter and poured the sauce over the chicken. She placed the platter at the head of the table where her father would sit. The cabbage noodles were placed in a large round bowl.

* * *

Chicken Paprikas Hungraise

2 frying chickens cut in quarters
1 large onion, chopped
1 chopped tomato
1 green pepper, chopped
2 large garlic cloves, diced
Oil Salt Pepper
1 heaping tbsp. Hungarian paprika
1 or more cups water
Sour cream (optional)

Sauté:
In a heavy skillet, slowly sauté the onions in oil till caramelized, mixing frequently. In a separate skillet, sauté chicken pieces, turning when golden. Place vegetables on

onions; cook till transparent and place chicken pieces on vegetables with the paprika. Mix all well.

Simmer:

Add about a cup of water, simmer for about an hour till done. Check to see if a little more water is required.

To Serve:

When done, place chicken on a large platter, and sprinkle with chopped dill or parsley. As an option you may also whip one cup of sour cream or yogurt into the sauce and pour over chicken.

Chapter 2

Havana

Nicolas could not sleep. He was afraid to because he had told his friends, Joseph and Aaron, that they would meet at 1:00 A.M. at the edge of the town. He spoke to his mother before he went to bed and had told her he was leaving. He couldn't leave without saying good-bye to her. He asked her forgiveness and to please tell his father he loved him, but felt he had to find his own way.

It was midnight. A clear night. There were fast moving gray clouds partly covering the bright moon. He jumped out of bed, dressed quickly and took the small bag of bread, hard-boiled eggs and flask of wine Julia, the cook, packed for him. She would always put together something for him to eat. She knew Nicolas would like to ride through the countryside and meet and talk to people in the fields; asking them if they needed anything. They all loved him. She made sure he ate well.

He paused for a moment and noticed a small, black leather-bound book partly hidden in his bag. It was his mother's bible that she would take to the synagogue with her on Saturday mornings. He kissed the bible and stuffed it in the bottom of his bag. He left a note for his father on his desk.

Tonight, he felt different. Tonight, he and his restless friends were ready to leave their home and country and head to the passage to their future. They had heard about a ship leaving from southern Yugoslavia for Spain and from there to America. They couldn't stop talking about America, "The Golden Land." Tonight was the night.

Nicolas tiptoed out to the stable, quietly reassuring Gypsy, saddled and mounted him. He rode the three miles towards the village where his friends were already waiting on their horses.

* * *

Together, they rode towards the end of their village, Szeged, and passed the synagogue where they had gone to school almost all their lives. Intent on their journey, they remained silent. They headed southwest along the Hungarian boundary, careful not to go into Romania. Since the Great War the two countries did not have good relations.

It seemed as though they had ridden all night, but it was about 40 miles. They headed towards Pecs, then a few more miles where they crossed the border into Yugoslavia. There, they stopped to rest their horses and themselves. Refreshed, they mounted and headed south. Their destination was the city of Split, a lovely city situated on the Adriatic Sea about 200 miles south of Pecs. There, they would beg passage on a ship and work their way toward Spain where they had heard that ships would leave for America regularly.

They spent a short while in Pecs and found someone to buy their horses. Nicolas felt sad when he sold Gypsy. They found working passage on one of the ships going to Barcelona, on the Mediterranean Sea.

From Barcelona the ship headed toward Havana, Cuba. They were told they would have to wait to obtain papers for America.

* * *

Havana was hot and humid, a busy city with over 1 million people, with narrow streets in the old section of town. There were shops, cafes, restaurants, apartments and outdoor markets with people strolling.

The men settled in a small hotel and set out to find work. They kept walking towards a small clump of tall palm trees and found themselves entering a park-like area with terrazzo floors and marble benches and palm trees and flowers. Lining the side of this park, which later they found out was called "The Prado," there were shops and businesses and restaurants. They saw a sign above one of the restaurants, "Café Swiss" and decided to go in. It was cool inside. The ceiling fans were twirling and under each one, the long sticky rolls of fly paper hung from each fan, with the dead flies stuck to them.

Nicolas smelled the aroma of familiar foods. He suddenly remembered he was hungry. From the back of the dining room appeared a short, bespectacled man with a hunched back. He smiled at them and ushered them to a table. Joseph and Aaron hesitated, but Nicolas sat down and took a menu. He noted some Hungarian dishes.

They ordered the "Hungarian goulash" with "nockel."

* * *

Hungarian Goulash with Nockel

1½ lbs. cubed chuck beef.
2 chopped onion
1 clove garlic, diced
1 tbsp. paprika.

1 green pepper, chopped
1 tomato, chopped Pinch of caraway seeds Salt
Pepper
4 or 5 potatoes, cubed

Sauté:
Brown beef. Add onion and garlic and mix.

Simmer:
Add water to cover. Simmer 1½ hour.
Add chopped pepper and tomato; caraway seeds; salt and pepper to taste.
Cover and simmer on low 1 ½ hour. Then add potatoes and simmer another ½ hour.

* * *

Nockel (Spatzle) Small Dumplings

Make a thick batter of 1/2 cup flour; water; 1 egg and salt. Drop by teaspoons in boiling salt water and simmer a few minutes, mixing at times. Remove as they come to the surface. Serve on the side with pad of butter and dill.

* * *

Herr Otto stood at the back of the dining room as he watched the three young men eating their meal. He smiled because he knew they were not natives or tourists. By the way they were eating he knew they were starving. He also knew they needed jobs. He remembered when he first landed in Havana from Austria after the Great War and began working as a dishwasher.

Nicolas was the first to finish eating. He always ate fast and was the first to leave the table. He went straight to Herr Otto and looking at him straight in his eyes said in Hungarian,

"Sir, we are three strong men and need jobs. Can you help us out?" Herr Otto liked this young man. He could use him in the dining room as a waiter and soon he'll learn Spanish, although his restaurant was visited often with international tourists. The other two boys can help out in the kitchen.

So, soon the three friends settled in. Nicolas took to his job easily. He had a good personality, was intelligent and learned quickly. They all worked hard and found a small apartment in town. He learned from Herr Otto how to greet, recommend the daily special dishes and how to serve the customer properly. The restaurant was very busy and Joseph and Aaron were also promoted to serve the customers.

The cuisine was mostly Austrian/German and Hungarian. They had a German chef and that was his name. No one knew his real name so they called him "Chef." His wife was heavyset, tall and very quiet but was constantly moving and working. Her strudels and coffee cakes were delicious. When it was time to make the strudels, Gretl would call Nicolas to help her stretch and drape the dough over the cloth-covered table, fill it with the fillings, roll and bake it.

Even though his days and nights were full of the work he loved, in the back of his mind his dream of going to America did not die and now, a new hope arose within him. He wanted to one day have his own restaurant business.

Chapter 3

It was fall of 1923-24. Maria, soon to be 20, sat by the fire. The days were getting shorter and colder and sadder, she thought. Her dear father had died the past summer. Her mother, burdened with the farm, and all the chores which had to be done, was courted by the widower, Mr. Popp, who was the village butcher and had four young children.

Teresa had no choice but to consider marriage, sell the farm, marry Mr. Popp and move into his large home in the village where she would have a maid and her children would go to the village school and get a good education.

Teresa's brother Matyas had been talking to her and advising her that this would be the best for her and her family. He soon would be leaving the country, hoping to go to America by way of Havana.

When Maria heard he was leaving the country, she ran crying to him and begged him to take her with him. She couldn't stay to see her mother re-married. After speaking with his sister, Uncle Matyas agreed. Soon, Maria began to pack the few handmade clothes she had and the embroidered doilies and pillowcases she had made for her dowry, one day. Teresa made her famous stuffed cabbage and served it to her family to say farewell to her brother and daughter.

* * *

Stuffed Cabbage

1 large cabbage, cored and boiled in salted water
2 large onions
1 lb. sauerkraut
1 14 oz. can of canned tomato sauce
1 8 oz. can whole cranberries
(or substitute Olga's addition: 1/2 cup brown sugar)
2 apples, sliced
1 large link pork or turkey sausage
1½ lbs. ground beef (can substitute ground turkey)
½ cup raw rice
Salt and pepper to taste
1 egg
chopped parsley
2-4 cups cabbage water

Boil:
Boil cabbage approximately 20 minutes and begin removing outer leaves as they soften. Cool, trim off center ribs from leaves so they will lay flat and place on platter.

Mix together:
Mix the meats, rice, egg and ½ of the chopped onion with salt and pepper to taste in a bowl.
Slice the rest of the onion and the center of the cabbage (where the leaves are small) set aside.

Stuff:
Place a large tbsp. of meat mixture in center of each leaf and form the cabbage rolls firmly, setting them aside.

Simmer:

Mix the tomato sauce and cranberry sauce in a separate small pot, bring to a simmer and correct seasoning (add sugar to sweeten if you like).

Sauté:

In a large heavy casserole, place sausage on bottom and sauté until golden.

Layer:

Layer the rest of the ingredients: Place a row of the larger rolls on the bottom of pan; sprinkle the sliced onions, cabbage and sauerkraut over them. Pour on a cupful of tomato sauce mixture and one sliced apple; then another row of cabbage rolls, sprinkle other ingredients. When done layering, pour the sauce over and top with sliced apples.

Shake the pan to distribute evenly. You can use the sauerkraut water and cabbage water to add to the casserole if too dry.

Boil, then Bake:

Cover and bring to a boil on top of stove for 15 minutes, then place in a 350° oven for 1 ½ hours, shaking casserole now and then to mix the juices. Uncover for the last 10 to 15 minutes.

Taste for seasoning

Serve with parsley seasoned boiled potatoes.

Chapter 4

Cuba

U ncle Matyas and Maria were in a taxi heading towards the outskirts of Havana. He had a friend in Hungary whose brother, a successful businessman trading in the famous Cuban cigars had been looking for a governess. His wife was in her eighth month of pregnancy and they had six young daughters, all under the age of seven. Maria would only take care of the newborn child, as there was other help in the household. Maria's uncle thought this would be a good opportunity for her as she was a stranger in a strange land.

Soon, they arrived. Maria, never, in her wildest dreams, ever saw a home like this one. The family was a lively, happy one and the mistress of the home welcomed her with open arms.

They showed her to her room. It was a large room with a balcony overlooking the gardens in the back of the house and, next to it, the nursery for the unborn child. They left her alone for a short while. She unpacked the few contents of her small suitcase, and noted a folded-up white cloth — that she had not packed — in the center of the case. She reached for it and saw that it was an embroidered handkerchief. She unfolded it and there in the center, were her mother's rosary beads. Sobbing, she walked over to a small table and sat down. She noticed some writing paper, and a pen and ink. She wrote her mother a letter, thanking her and telling her of the wonderful family she was with and the beautiful home she would be living in.

Maria went down an elegant staircase and the children, who had been waiting at the bottom of the stairs, ran to her laughing and giggling. Holding her hands and pulling her skirt, they led her to the dining room and sat her down at a long table, which held the entire family, two other governesses plus Maria and her uncle. Everyone quieted down, clasped their hands and bowed their heads. Senor Farpon recited grace. Then, Senora Farpon rang a little bell and Maria's first Cuban dinner was served.

* * *

Arroz Con Pollo (Chicken with Rice)

For the marinade, mix together:
3 cloves garlic
1 tsp. salt
½ tsp. pepper
Add ¼ cup orange juice and ¼ cup lime juice. Pour mixture on to a 4 lb. cut up chicken in a glass bowl. Cover and refrigerate 1 to 1 ½ hours. Save the marinade.
Brown Chicken:
Brown the chicken on both sides in 2 tbsp. vegetable oil in heavy skillet. Place on a dish, set aside.

Sauté:
2 chopped onions
1 chopped green pepper in same pan

Add:
3 cups chicken broth

3 strands saffron
¼ cup tomato sauce
Marinade chicken

Simmer:
Simmer 30 minutes.

Add:
2 cups short grain rice
31/2 cups water
Add rice and stir. If too dry, add 1 cup of beer or white wine.

Boil:
Bring to a boil.
Cover and steam gently for about 30 minutes. Add more wine or beer if too dry.

To Serve:
Place chicken on the outer rim of a large platter and the rice in the center.
Decorate the top with small Spanish olives, slices of pimiento or little peas (petit pois). Serve with tomato avocado salad and Platanos Fritos.

* * *

Tomato/Avocado Salad

2 large ripe quartered tomatoes
2 avocados quartered
Thinly sliced onions
1 lemon juiced
Olive oil Salt Pepper
Mix all ingredients to make salad.

* * *

Platanos Fritos (fried plantains)
Platanos Verdes (green plaintains)

3 green plantains dry
Peel and slice into ½ inch rounds. Fry in ½ inch of oil till golden and drain. Place in paper bag to absorb oil. Remove from bag then mash and refry one minute until golden. Drain on paper towel, salt and serve.

* * *

Platanos Maduros (ripe)

3 yellow plantains
Peel and cut into 1-inch slices. Fry in ½ inch oil on both sides until golden, drain and serve. Sprinkle with sugar (optional).

* * *

Maria became very close to Senora Farpon. They would sit on the shaded veranda before the hot noon sun would appear, talking with much gesturing and with dictionaries in their hands. Maria was slowly learning Spanish and Senora Farpon would bring her into their large kitchen, introduce her to Carmela, their cook, and as Carmela prepared her dishes, Maria would watch and sometimes help her. She loved being in the kitchen, which reminded her of the days at home, helping her mother.

Senora Farpon would also show Maria the different plates, platters and silverware the food would be served on. Also, the lovely Spanish embroidered linens, which would be used for the family and for company.

She was happy in her new surroundings and looked forward to the birth of the new baby.

Chapter 5

Café Cubano

Café Swiss was very busy. Nicolas would work seven days a week from early morning till late at night. Herr Otto did not know what he would do without him. He felt as though Nicolas was his son and gave him every chance to earn money. Joseph and Aaron had left the restaurant, one to try his luck with a small jeweler on the Prado and the other in the exporting of the Cuban cigars.

Nicolas liked the restaurant business and had a deep desire to own one himself. He had been saving money and felt he would be ready soon to make his step. He had been in Havana for almost two years. It was 1926. Havana was a leading tourist attraction for the Europeans and the wealthy Americans. The political climate was unstable, but the government welcomed the tourist dollars. He felt that if he had to work so many hours, he might as well work for himself.

Herr Otto was thinking about Nicolas one day and spoke to him after the lunch hour, when it quieted down during siesta time. "Miklos," he called him by his Hungarian name, "I look at you every day and wonder how you can go on working so many hours without a little recreation. You are a young man and need to find some young people to have a little fun. The Hungarian Club in old Havana is having a social dance and I'm giving you time off to go."

"But!" said Nicolas.

"No buts, you go and don't come in tomorrow. Pepe and Jose will manage and need be, Gretl will be the hostess!"

They both laughed at that. Gretl was hard-working, but they never saw a smile on her face. Not a good disposition for a hostess.

Nicolas slept late the next morning. He didn't realize how exhausted he had been. It was after 1:00 P.M. he showered, got dressed and went to get a haircut. Then he stopped into a men's shop, bought a pair of light linen slacks and a shirt, put them on in the shop and left his other clothes to be washed and pressed. He walked along Calle Viega where he had his apartment. His two friends had moved out earlier in the year. He kept walking past the markets and the apartments and he found himself in a street with palm trees and flowers lining the walks. In front of him at the corner was a café. Small tables with umbrellas and chairs surrounded the storefront and two huge urns filled with crimson red flowers of the Bougainvillea vines trailing up the facade of the restaurant. Above the front door was a small wooden sign that read "Cafe Cubano."

Nicolas went in. There was a long bar on the right and wooden tables and chairs to the left. Past the bar, to the right there were four large wooden shutter doors, open to a stone patio where six tables and umbrellas were placed.

He called for attention and an elderly woman came out. "Si Senor? Querer a comer?" (Would you like to eat?) Nicolas nodded and sat down. There was no menu.

He sat for about 10 minutes and the old lady came out with a large platter and following her, an elderly gentleman with a large bowl and a basket of hot crusty Cuban bread. They set the dishes on the table in front of Nicolas and went behind the bar. In front of Nicolas there was a large platter of Picadillo and white rice. The elderly man brought him a large ice-cold glass of beer and disappeared behind the bar once more. The old lady brought him a soup tureen with a ladle in it.

Nicolas had never eaten anything so delicious and satisfying.

* * *

Picadillo with White Rice
(Seasoned Ground Meat Sauce)

1 onion, chopped
1 green pepper, chopped
3 cloves garlic
1 lb. lean ground beef or half ground pork and beef
2 oz. tomato sauce
4 oz. stuffed small green olives
4 oz. raisins
1 tbsp. capers
2 tbsp. white vinegar
1tsp sugar
1 tsp. salt
Pepper

Sauté:
Sauté 1 chopped onion and 1 chopped green pepper in olive oil. Add 3 diced cloves of garlic. Do not burn garlic.

Add:
1 lb. lean ground beef or half ground pork and half beef.
Mix well and cook until meat loses its red color.
Stir in 2 ounces tomato sauce, stuffed small green olives, raisins; capers, white vinegar, sugar, salt and pepper

Simmer:

Cover and simmer gently for about ½ hour, stirring at times.

To Serve:
Serve on a large platter with white rice and the black beans on the side.
Garnish with small peas and/or pimiento strips.

* * *

Black Bean Soup

1 lb. dry black beans or 2 to 3 cans of black beans
1 green pepper, sliced
½ onion
2 garlic cloves, crushed
1 tsp. salt
½ tsp. pepper

Soak Dry Beans:
Rinse 1 pound black beans in colander. Soak overnight, covered with water. Skip this step if using canned beans.

Boil and Simmer:
In a heavy pot, boil the beans till soft, 1 to 1 ½ hrs.
adding 1 sliced green pepper, ½ chopped onion, 2 crushed garlic cloves, 1 tsp. salt, ½ tsp. pepper.
Lower heat to simmer, cover and cook. Skim the foam at times.

Making the Sofrito:
2 onions, chopped
1 green pepper, chopped
5-6 cloves garlic, diced
Salt
Pepper

½ tsp. cumin
½ tsp. oregano
1 bay leaf
1 tbsp. sugar
2 tbsp. white vinegar
2 tbsp. olive oil

Sauté:
In a heavy skillet, sauté chopped onions, chopped green pepper a few minutes. Add garlic cloves, salt, pepper, cumin and oregano, bay leaf and sugar.

Serving the Soup:
Remove the bay leaf, add the sofrito, white vinegar and olive oil and serve.

This may be served as a first course as a soup with chopped raw onion and diced avocado on top of bowl or it may be served over the white rice as a main dish.

* * *

Dessert

Platter of compote de guayava (guava) Queso Blanca (white cheese)
Galleticas (Crackers)
Café Liqueur Cafe Negro Demitasse

He pushed his chair back and found it difficult to get up from the table. Nicolas wasn't used to eating a full course meal. He was always too busy to sit down and when he did, it would be a delicious one-dish meal Chef would serve him. He would eat it fast and continue working. But this meal was eaten at a leisurely pace, savoring every mouthful.

He stood up, went to the bar, smiled at the couple and said, in his limited Spanish, "Estava muy sabroso." (It was very delicious.) He paid for his meal and walked the half hour or so to his apartment, where he threw himself down on the bed and fell asleep.

* * *

When Nicolas woke up, it was almost dark. He quickly washed his face and went out into the street. He hailed a cab and rode almost an hour to the area where the Hungarian Club was holding its weekly dance.

He heard the sounds of the familiar Hungarian czardas, a lively Hungarian dance. He was surprised to see so many young people dancing and sitting at the tables on the side. He looked around and saw his two friends and at the same time, they saw him. They walked towards each other and hugged, happy to see each other. They were both doing well in their chosen professions. The music began again, the two young men went looking for some dance partners and Nicolas stood, watching the dancers.

He looked around and his eyes caught a young lady, sitting by herself. She had dark chestnut colored hair and was lovely to look at. Nicolas felt as though he knew her. She turned her head and looked at him. He couldn't stop staring at her and she couldn't turn her eyes from him.

She watched him walk toward her, gasped, and felt she couldn't take another breath. She felt as if the young man with the dark, curly hair and soft brown eyes and warm smile was walking toward her in slow motion.

Nicolas walked slowly towards her, his heart beating wildly. He looked into her hazel, gold-flecked eyes and the feeling he had once before felt returned. They could not tear their eyes away from each other. Nicolas asked in Hungarian, "Do I know you? Have we met before?"

She looked into his eyes, and answered "Nicolas, I am Maria and I gave you the water which you drank with the Sunday Ladle."

Chapter 6

Love

Maria left the dance hall soon after meeting Nicolas. The Farpon's driver was outside waiting for her. On the way home, the strange feelings deep within her, which she had had before when she first met Nicolas, resurfaced.

It was difficult for her to sleep and it was just as well because Enrique, the Farpon's son, who was now 18 months old, had awakened and called out to her. She went to him, held him and rocked him back to sleep while singing him a little song she learned. "Duerme te mi hijoto, duerme te mi amor."

The Farpons had been hoping for a son to follow the six daughters they had. When Enrique was born there was great happiness in the household and Jose Farpon had a large party with close to 500 people attending.

Maria bonded with the baby as well as his mother. The Farpons treated Maria as one of their own and trusted her to care for their only son.

One day, Christina Farpon called for her and said "Maria, you have been constantly attending to Enrique for the past 18 months without a break. You are a young girl and need a social life." That is when she told Maria of the dance in the city and made plans for her to go with her chauffeur who would take her and wait for her to bring her back home.

Maria placed Enrique back in his crib, sat in the semi- dark nursery on the rocking chair and cried herself to sleep. When the first morning light entered the room, Enrique woke up laughing and happy to see her sitting on the rocker. Senora Farpon came in, lifted the baby from the crib and asked Maria about the dance. "It was alright," she answered and left the room.

That afternoon, she was sitting on the shaded veranda while Enrique was napping and Senora Farpon came to her and sat beside her. She asked what was the matter and Maria began to sob while telling her of her feelings for the young man who had reentered her life once more, and the difference in their religions, ending with "I'll never go back to that dance hall again." Senora Farpon smiled and reassured the lonely girl.

"This is a once-in-a-lifetime event for you. To have come almost halfway around the world and again find the one person who had stirred your heart years later, is almost like a miracle. You must go back!" she told Maria.

When Senora Farpon recounted the story to her husband the next evening, he said, "Give her time, then she must go back to the dance hall once more. If the young man will be there, then it will be the will of God."

Maria could not think of going back. The Farpons waited patiently, then four weeks later Maria finally came to them and said she would go back with Delia, the other young governess.

The dance hall was just as crowded as before. The music loud and lively. Delia danced with several young men and Maria refusing those who asked her. She sat at the same small table as before. She did see Nicolas' two friends. Aaron came over and said hello, then left. After about an hour, she was ready to leave and stood up to look for Delia who was laughing and dancing with a small group of young people. She felt a tap on her shoulder, turned, and there he was.

* * *

When Nicolas saw her the first time he had come to the dance his heart flipped.

At first, he did not recognize her. It was almost three years since he left Hungary. He was 25 years old and Maria had matured from a 20-year-old shy farm girl to a lovely 23-year-old young lady. Since that time he couldn't stop thinking about her.

He came every week for the entire month, but she was not there. He didn't know her address and no one else knew her. His mind wasn't on his work and even Herr Otto noticed. "What's the matter with you? Miklos. This is not you." Then Nicolas told him and Herr Otto said, "keep going back and she will turn up."

It was the end of the month and Nicolas didn't want to be disappointed again. He left the restaurant late, hailed a cab and left for the dance hall. That is when he saw her. They sat and talked for a long time until slowly the lights dimmed and everyone was ushered out. He asked Maria for her address and she gave it to him. He watched her going into the car and Delia following her laughing and giggling.

* * *

It was difficult for Maria to concentrate on her thoughts. Delia kept jabbering away talking about this young fellow and that one and the dancing and she couldn't wait to go back next week.

Maria's heart was full. She knew if she saw Nicolas again that their friendship would get more serious. They were of two different religions and she knew their families would oppose the relationship. She decided not to go back to the dance hall. The next morning she told Mrs. Farpon and Mrs. Farpon said, "Maria, follow your heart." That evening, Maria took her mother's rosary beads, prayed, put them back in the embroidered handkerchief, and put it away in the back of the bureau drawer.

Nicolas felt as though he was the happiest person in the entire world. After this meeting with Maria, he felt as though his entire world would change. They had so many things in common. They came from the same country; their villages were only 20 miles apart; they spoke the same language; they enjoyed the same type of food; he felt if he didn't see her again that it would be the end of the world; he felt that he was in love with Maria Takacz — except for the fact that they were born into two different religions.

He thought about her as he worked; and as he greeted the customers in the restaurant; as he ordered the supplies for Chef; but it always came back to the love he felt for Maria and he felt this love would carry them through life.

He couldn't wait to see her again and when he went back to the dance hall he went early and waited for her, but she never came. It was the same thing the next week and the next. Finally, he could wait no longer. He called a cab and they rode to the Marianao area of the city. He went up to the front door and rang the bell. A maid opened the door and he asked for Maria. She came down the staircase, they ran towards each other and hugged and kissed.

Chapter 7

Wedding

Maria and Nicolas were married at the Justice of the Peace's office in downtown Havana. Their reception was hosted by Herr Otto in the Cafe Swiss, and he invited the Farpons and their entire family. Delia tried to hold onto little Enrique's hand most of the time. Joseph and Aaron were there as well as several loyal customers of the restaurant who had befriended Nicolas.

Pepe and Jose served the buffet luncheon and Chef and Gretl outdid themselves with the dishes that were served. Even Gretl smiled when she served the platter of:

Baked Red Snapper

One 6 to 7 lb. snapper
1/3 cup lime juice
5 cloves garlic, minced
2 tsp. salt
1 tsp. oregano
1 onion, sliced
1 green pepper, sliced

2 bay leaves
½ cup olive oil
pinch of black pepper
2 tbsp. wine vinegar
1 cup tomato sauce
2 tbsp. white wine

Marinade:
Pour lime juice over fish & set aside on a glass (or non-reactive) dish.
Mash together garlic, salt and oregano and rub marinade inside fish.

Layer:
Layer ½ sliced onion and ½ sliced green pepper on bottom with 2 bay leaves, pinch of pepper; ½ cup olive oil.
Place fish on top of vegetables. Sprinkle 2 tbsp. wine vinegar and 1 cup tomato sauce over fish.
Place other halves of sliced onion and green pepper and 2 bay leaves over fish; pour about 2 tbsp. white wine, ½ cup olive oil and a pinch of pepper over fish.

Bake:
Cover loosely with foil and bake 35 minutes. Remove foil and bake 10 more minutes.

To Serve:
Serve on a large, deep platter with chopped parsley and the juices poured over all.

* * *

Strudel

Use ready made filo dough from the market and follow directions for use
Sweet butter, melted
bread crumbs (unflavored)
1 egg, beaten
Place 5 sheets filo dough on a large kitchen towel. Sprinkle each sheet one at a time with melted sweet butter, then unflavored bread crumbs. Place filling on dough and roll with the help of the kitchen towel until the edge is at the bottom of the long roll.

Place the roll on a well-buttered cookie sheet, press down slightly and sprinkle top with more melted butter. Brush top with a beaten egg.

Bake at 375° 25 to 30 minutes till golden brown. Sprinkle with powdered sugar and serve warm.

* * *

Apple Filling

2 lbs. golden apples mixed with Granny Smith, sliced thin.
½ cup raisins
1 cup sugar
1 tsp. cinnamon
1 cup grated walnuts
½ cup bread crumbs
1 tbsp. grated lemon rind
Mix together for filling.

***

Cherry Filling

1 can cherry filling

3 tbsp. cherry liquor
1 cup sugar
1 cup walnuts, grated
1 tbsp. tapioca
Drain 1 can cherry filling, unsweetened, and mix in 3 tbsp. cherry liqueur. Mix 1 cup sugar; 1 cup grated walnuts; 1tbs. tapioca. Place on dough.

* * *

Chef made many dishes, stuffed cabbage, chicken paprikas, black bean soup with white rice, flan and omelets.

* * *

Individual Spanish Omelets

2 tbsp. olive oil
1 onion, sliced
1 lb. Italian sweet peppers, sliced
3 large ripe tomatoes, chopped
½ tbsp. sugar
½ tbsp. salt
1 tbsp. paprika
2 eggs per serving

Filling (Lecho)
Sauté sliced onion in olive oil slowly. Add sliced sweet red peppers and cook for 10 minutes.
   Add peeled and chopped tomatoes, sugar, salt, and paprika and sauté 10 more minutes together with rest of vegetables.

Omelet:
Make individual 2 egg omelets in small skillet.
Fill with the Lecho, roll and place them individually next to each other on a platter.

* * *

Caramel Custard (Flan)

2/3 cup sugar
1 tsp. vanilla
4 eggs
1¾ cups hot milk
5 tbsp. sugar
1 tbsp. water

Custard:
Mix sugar, vanilla and eggs. Whisk together, add milk slowly and gently whisk constantly.

Caramel:
5 tbsp. sugar; 1 tbsp. water.
In a small frying pan melt sugar and water on low heat. Do not mix, shake pan until golden.

Pour into mold:
Pour into cake mold with at least 2 inch sides turning, with pot holders, so bottom and sides are covered with the caramel.
Pour custard into pan. Place pan into a larger pan of hot water. (Water should come to ½ the side of the cake pan.)

Bake:
Bake in a pre-heated oven at 350° for 40 to 45 minutes.
Test for doneness with a knife. If the knife is clean, the custard is done.

Refrigerate.
When cool, place platter on top of custard and turn custard unto a large platter with at least a two-inch rim to hold the caramel sauce.

Chapter 8

Restaurant Budapest

*Nicolas Weiss, in tuxedo, and his uncle Josi
in front of Restaurant Budapest.*

They were very happy. Nicolas worked his long hours at the restaurant and Maria tried to work around his hours too. The Farpons' driver would pick her up and take her to be with little Enrique for a few hours so she could give him dinner, bathe him, then put him to sleep. She would then rush back to their little apartment and wait for Nicolas after the dinner hour.

Nicolas would tell her of his dream of owning his own restaurant. Maria kept encouraging him. One day, he went to Herr Otto and told him what he wanted to do and of a small place he thought would be the perfect one, except he didn't think he had enough money.

Herr Otto said, "Take me to this place." So, they went together to Café Cubano. They entered. It was dark and cool inside. The fans were whirling, the wooden shuttered doors to the terrace were closed and the caned wooden chairs were turned upside down on all the tables except the one near the long bar. The old man was seated at that table with his head bent on his arms, fast asleep.

Herr Otto patted the man's shoulder and he woke up. He greeted them, stood up and motioned them to sit down. He went behind the bar and brought out two tall glasses of beer and set them down before the men.

They thanked him and asked him to sit with them. Herr Otto asked him, point blank, if he wanted to sell his place. The old man looked at them both, took a deep breath and said yes. He stood up, ran to the back and brought his wife with him. They were laughing and crying at the same time. They were too old to keep the business and had no one to help them run it.

The four of them settled on a fair price. Nicolas had Herr Otto as a partner with Nicolas running the restaurant. Herr Otto knew he had a good partner, although he thought it would be difficult to fill Nicolas' shoes at the Café Swiss.

* * *

Once they finalized the legalities of the sale, they left their respective employers and concentrated on their new project. Nicolas began with the kitchen and hired a young man, Antonio, who had some knowledge of cooking. Together, they ripped out the old stove and icebox and with help from Herr Otto's friend bought new equipment. They scrubbed the kitchen and painted it. They decided to use the same dishes but added new serving pieces and glassware.

Maria concentrated on the dining room and terrace. She hired Delia's sister, Dora, to help her and together, they washed the tables and chairs and scrubbed the terrazzo floors and ceiling fans. White linen cloths were placed on the tables and small glass vases of fresh flowers.

Nicolas's friend, Joseph, stopped in and asked if he had a job for his brother who had been working in Vienna as a chef's helper for a few years. Nicolas couldn't believe this stroke of luck. Together, with Maria and Edmond, the new cook, and Antonio, they sat down to figure out the new menu for:

Restaurant Budapest
Little Hungary
O'Reilly 82, Esq. a Vellegas
Telefono M-8768

This is the menu for Restaurant Budapest, Nicolas and Maria's first business, which opened in Havana in June of 1928.

ENTREMES

Cocktail de Frutas 30
Toronja con Marraquino 10
Cocktail de Guayriche 40
Cocktail de Camarones 40
Langua fría 30
Pavo frío 30
Jamón frío 30
Entremés surtido 35
Canapé Caviar 50
Anchoas 30
Sardinas en aceite 30
Aceitunas 10
Apio 20

SOPAS

Consomme caliente 10
Consomme frío 10
Tortuga (2 huevos) 40
Crema de Espárragos 30
Crema de Tomate 30
Legumbres 30

HUEVOS

Fritos (2) 20
Pasados (2) 15
Al Plato (2) 20
Malagueña 35
Con Jamón o Tocineta 35
Tortilla 25
" con Papas 30
" con Petit Pois 35
" con cebollas 30
" con Queso 35
" Champiñón 45
con Hígado de Pollo 40
Revoltillo con Sesos 40

PESCADOS Y MARISCOS

Filete de Pargo Frito 30
Pargo Menadero 35
Pescado al estilo Húngaro 35
Langosta Mayonesa 30
Langosta Grille 30
Langosta a la Catalana 40
Langosta a la Newborough 40
Cangrejo enchilado 45
Camarones a la Catalana 40
Camarones a la Bordelesa 40

AVES

Pollo Guisado estilo Húngaro . . 60
Pollo a la Maryland 50
Pollo Casserole 50
Pollo grillé o frito 60
Arroz con Pollo 60
Pavo Asado con Cranberry 60

ENTRANTES

Gulash Húngaro 35
Lengua a la Italiana 35
Hígado de Pollo frito 40
Riñón Sauté 35

ASADOS

Steak a la Budapest 40
Beefsteak Hamburguesa 30
Ternera Vienesa 35
Ternera a la Holstein 30
Escalope de Ternera 30
Costilla de Puerco frita 30
Costilla de Puerco a la Budapest 35
Filete Mignon a la Budapest . . . 50
Beefsteak de Filete 50
Steak de Hígado con Tocineta . . 40

LEGUMBRES

Espinaca 15
Habichuela 15
Petit Pois 15
Zanahoria 10
Col agria 10
Plátano frito 10
Papas Guisadas 10
" Puré 10
" Alemana 15
" Fritas 15
" a la Saratoga 15
" a la Juliana 15
" Lyonase 15

PASTAS

Macarrones a la Italiana 30
Macarrones a la Caruso 30
Espaguetis a la Napolitana 30
Espaguetis en Salsa Crema 30

ENSALADAS

Lechuga, Tomate, Remolacha . . 10
Aguacate, Berros 15
Mixta 15
Espárragos 25
Pollo 35
Langosta 35, Cangrejo y Camarones 45

POSTRES

Flanco Húngaro con Mermelada 20
Helado en Copa de Vino 35
Flan de Leche 10
Pastel Francés 10
Pudín Diplomático 10
Frutas en conserva 30
Frutas de Estación 30
Helados 10

QUESOS

Crema de Queso de Guayaba . . . 15
Gruyere 15
Roquefort 15
Limburger 15
Camembert 20

SANDWICHES

Club 0.60
Pollo o Pavo 35
Jamón y Queso 35
Lechuga y Tomate 25

CAFE, TE, ETC

Café con Leche 10
Café con Crema 15
Demi Tasse 5
Chocolate 10
Cocoa 10
Te caliente o frío 5
Leche fría 10

RELISHES

Fruit Cocktail 30
Grape Fruit with Marraschino . . 10
Moro Grain Cocktail 40
Shrimps Cocktail 40
Lobster Cocktail 30
Cold Beef Tongue 30
Cold Turkey 40
Cold Ham 30
Assorted Cold Meats 35
Canape Caviar 40
Anchovies 30
Oil Sardines 30
Green Olives 10
Celery 20

SOUPS

Hot Consomme 10
Cold Consomme 15
Turtle (2 Eggs) 40
Asparagus Cream 30
Tomatoes Cream 30
Vegetables 30

EGGS

Fried (2) 20
Boiled (2) 15
Shirred (2) 20
Malagueña 35
With Ham or Bacon 35
Spanish 25
Omelet 25
Potatoes 30
Green Peas 35
Onions 30
Cheese 35
Mush Room 45
Chicken Liver 40
Scrambled Eggs with Brain 40

SEA FOODS

Fried Filets of Redsnapper 30
Red Snapper Menavera 35
Fish Hungarian Style 35
Lobster Mayonnaise 30
Lobster Grille 30
Lobster Spanish Style 40
Lobster a la Newborough 40
Moro Crab with Tartar Sauce . . 45
Moro Crab Mexican Style 45
Moro Crab Spanish Style 40
Shrimps Bordelaise 40

POULTRY

Hungarian Chicken Stew 60
Chicken a la Maryland 50
Chicken in Casserole 50
Broiled or fried Chicken 60
Chicken with Rice 60
Roast Turkey with Cranberry Sauce 60

ENTREES

Hungarian Goulash 35
Tongue Italian Style 35
Fried Chicken Liver w. Onions . 40
Kidneys Sauté 35

ROAST

Budapest Steak 40
Hamburger Steak with Onions . 35
Wiener Schnitzel 35
Holstein Schnitzel 30
Veal Escalope 30
Fried Pork Chops 30
Pork Chops a la Budapest 35
Filet Mignon a la Budapest 35
Tenderloin Steak 50
Fried Liver with Bacon 40

VEGETABLES

Spinach 15
String Bean 15
Green Peas 15
Carrot 10
Sauerkraut 10
Fried Banana 10
Boiled " Potatoes 10
Mashed " 10
German Fried 15
French Fried 15
Saratoga 15
Julienne 15
Lyonaise 15

ITALIAN DISHES

Macaroni Italian Style 30
Macaroni Caruso Style 30
Spaghetti a la Napolitan 30
Spaghetti with Cream Sauce . . . 30

SALADS

Lettuce, Tomatoes, Red Beets . . 10
Alligator Pear, Watercress 15
Mixed 15
Asparagus 25
Chicken 35
Lobster 35, Moro Crab 45, Shrimps 40

DESSERTS

Hungarian Pudding w. Marmalade 20
Iden with Wine Cream 35
Cup Custard 10
French Pastry 10
Diplomatic Pudding 10
Assorted Preserved Fruits 30
Fruits in Season 30
Ice Cream 10

CHEESE

Cream with guava preserved . . . 15
Gruyere 15
Roquefort 15
Limburger 15
Camembert 20

SANDWICHES

Club 40
Chicken or Turkey 35
Ham or Cheese 35
Lettuce and Tomatoes 15
Onion 30

COFFEE, TEA, ETC

Coffee with Milk 10
Coffee with Cream 15
Demi Tasse 5
Chocolate 10
Cocoa 10
Hot or Cold Tea 5
Cold Milk 10

WINE LIST

COCKTAILS

Budapest	0.20
Martini	0.20
Presidente	0.20
Alexander	0.25
Bacardi	0.25
Bronx	0.25
Canadian Club	0.25
Daiquiri	0.25
Dubonnet	0.25
Gin	0.25
Manhattan	0.25
Mary Pickford	0.25
Pick Me Up	0.25
Pine Apple Blossom	0.25
Zazarac	0.25
Side Car	0.25
Clover Club	0.30
Old Fashion	0.35
Gin Fizz	0.30
Sloe Gin Fizz	0.30
Silver Fizz	0.35
Golden Fizz	0.35

VERMOUTHS

Ams, Brocchi, Cinzano or Nolly-Prat	0.15
Port, Sherry, Moscatel or Manzanilla	0.20

WHISKIES

Whisky Strait	0.20
High Balls with Mineral	0.25
High Balls with Ginger Ale	0.35

RUMS (Ronos)

Bacardi, Carta Blanca	0.10
Bacardi, Carta de Oro	0.15
Bacardi, 1873	0.20
Bacardi, Elixir	0.20
Negrita	0.20

BRANDIES (Coñacs)

Domecq (Tres Cepas)	0.15
Domecq (Fundador)	0.20
Hennessy, Three Stars	0.20
Martell, Three Stars	0.20

GINS (Ginebras)

Gordon Dry	0.20
Bols	0.20
Sloe	0.25

LIQUEURS (Licores)

Anis del Mono	0.15
Anisette	0.20
Apricot Brandy	0.20
Benedictine	0.20
Chartreuse green or yellow	0.20
Cherry Brandy	0.20
Cointreau	0.20
Crema Cacao	0.20
Crema de Menthe Verde	0.20
Curacao	0.20
Kirsch	0.20
Kummel	0.20
Grand Marnier	0.25
D'Or (Gold Water)	0.25
Bols d'Amour	0.25
Pousse Café	0.20
Pousse Bandera Húngara	0.30
Pousse 7 Colours	0.40

CHAMPAGNES

G. H. Mumm	6.00	3.00
Torley Reserve or Extra Dry (Húngaro)	6.00	
Gordon Rouge	6.00	3.00
Veuve Clicot	6.00	3.00

HUNGARIAN WINES (Vinos Húngaros)

Tokaj Furmint	1.80	1.00
Tokaj Szamorodni 1920	2.20	
Tokaj Szamorodni 1911	2.50	
Tokaj Szamorodni 1889	3.00	
Tokaj Aszu (Ausbruch) 1910	2.80	
Tokaj Aszu (Ausbruch) 1901	015 ltr. 0.80	

WHITE WINES (Vinos blancos)

Rioja Blanco	1.00	0.50
Castell de Remey	1.50	0.80
Haut Sauternes	1.50	0.80
Liebfraumilch	1.80	
White Wine with Siphon	0.20	

RED WINES (Vinos Tintos)

Rioja Clarete	1.00	0.50
Marqués de Riscal	1.50	0.80
Medoc	1.50	0.80
Saint Julien	1.50	
CIDERS (Sidras)	0.50	0.30

BEERS (Cervezas)

Big Class	0.10	
Small Glass	0.05	
Cristal, Hatuey, Polar or Tropical	0.10	
Maltina or Trimalta	0.15	
Pilsener Urquella	0.30	
Beck, Bremen (Llave)	0.30	
Ginger Ale	0.25	0.20
,, Split		0.15

MINERAL WATER

San Francisco or La Cotorra	0.10	0.05
Evian, 1 ltr.		
Po'and, 1 ltr.		

REFRESHMENTS (Refrescos)

Pine Apple Juice	0.10
Pure Orange Juice	0.10
Coca-Cola, Ironbeer, Orange-Crush, etc.	0.05

They worked on the menu for many days. Sometimes adding, sometimes deleting items according to market conditions. Finally, they all felt the restaurant was ready to open and in June of 1928 there was a grand opening. Herr Otto closed his restaurant and came with his staff to lend a hand.

They were very busy even though it was brutally hot. People ate and drank the cold beers and rum Rickeys. There was a roving violinist who went from table to table entertaining the guests.

Nicolas and Maria set up a rolling pastry cart with portions of all the pastries baked on the premises. The customers would choose what they wanted and the price would be added to their bill.

It was a long day. Even after the dinner closing hour of 10:00 P.M. people would still be lingering outdoors on the patio, sipping their drinks. It was a friendly atmosphere, and continued to be for the next few years.

Late that night, when they were finally in bed, Maria told Nicolas that she was expecting their first child in January. Nicolas was overjoyed. She hadn't been feeling very well lately, but held it back from Nicolas because of the long hours he had been putting in at the restaurant.

Nicolas didn't want Maria to come to the restaurant the next day. She stayed and rested and came in just before the dinner hour. She found that she enjoyed being in the kitchen, watching the Chef and Antonio put together their dishes. She learned many of their dishes, which were very familiar to her and she gave them many ideas and recipes which were her mother's.

* * *

As the weeks and months passed, Maria had a gnawing feeling. She kept thinking of the child within her and perhaps of more to come and of how they would be raised. She wanted to be able to answer their questions and be knowledgeable of her husband's culture. Nicolas wasn't worried and told her that they would teach them the good values of both religions.

During the 1920s and 1930s many immigrants left Europe in the hopes of entering America. They settled in Cuba. Many were Ashkenazi Jews from Russia, Hungary, and Germany. Many more were the Sephardic Jews from Turkey.

In the apartment next to theirs were a brother and sister from Hungary.

He had been a cantor in Budapest. Maria would sometimes come by and talk to them and one day she told Cantor Roth of her feelings about how she wanted to raise her children with one religion. She kept this feeling secret as she learned.

Cantor Roth began to teach her how to light the Friday night Sabbath candles and the prayer to recite over the two candles to usher in the one day of rest on Saturday. Maria felt close to this ritual as it reminded her of her mother lighting candles in church and their day of rest on Sunday. He taught her about the meal that was usually served on Friday nights after the men and children would come home from the synagogue.

Beginning with the Gefilte Fish, a cold chopped fish dish served with horseradish; accompanied by the Challah bread or twisted egg bread.

He taught her that the Sabbath came at the end of the 6-day workweek when one reads in the Bible that we must have one day of rest.

* * *

Gefilte Fish (Stuffed Fish)

3 lbs. filets of fish,
(but reserve the heads and tails for the broth)
½ pike and ½ white-fish or pike and carp
3 large onions
Salt
Pepper

1tsp. sugar
4½ cups water
1/2 cup Matzo meal
2 eggs
2 sliced carrots
Parsley
1 tsp. baking powder

Simmer:
Place fish heads and tails, two sliced onions, and seasonings in 4 cups boiling water; simmer 1 ½ hours.

Strain broth, place in a large pot bringing to a simmer.

Grind:
Place fish and one onion in food processor on pulse. Do not puree.

Mix:
Place in a bowl and add the eggs, ½ cup water, matzo meal, salt and pepper, sugar and chopped parsley Mix together.

Form into Balls:
Wet your hands, form oval balls (about two heaping tbsp.) and drop into broth. Add the carrots. Add about 1 cup of water if needed to cover fish.

Simmer:
Simmer gently about for 1½ hours, covered.

To Serve:
When done, place in a serving dish, top with carrots, cover with plastic wrap, and refrigerate to gel the broth. Serve cold with horseradish sauce or serve hot as a main dish with the broth.

Challah (Twisted Sabbath Yeast Bread)

8-8 ½ cups bread flour
1 tbsp. sugar
2 cups lukewarm water
2 packets dry yeast
2 tbsp. vegetable oil
¼ cup lukewarm water
1 tbsp. salt
2 eggs
(Recipe can be split in half to make two loaves instead of four.)

Mix Dough:
In a mixing bowl place oil, salt and water. Mix yeast in ½ cup lukewarm water separately. When bubbled, pour yeast in mixing bowl with rest of warm water and add beaten eggs and gradually the flour, mixing and stirring, then kneading until smooth and elastic. Use an electric mixer about ten minutes. Lightly oil a large mixing bowl, pour kneaded dough in, cover with a clean cloth and set aside in a warm place until it doubles in bulk.

Cut and Form Dough:
When dough has risen, turn out on a floured board, cut in quarters and each quarter cut in half. With each half make a braid by cutting three pieces of dough and rolling it into long strips. Form the larger pieces of dough, make a long roll and place the braid on top of the roll, ending with 4 challah breads. Brush entire bread twists with egg yolk and sprinkle with poppy seeds. Allow to rise until doubled in size.

Bake:
Bake for 15 minutes in a 400° oven, then lower to 350° for total of one hour.

Turn out on a board to cool. Then place two loaves on a large platter, cover with a linen napkin and place on the center of the Sabbath table.

Before the meal begins, a piece of the Challah is broken off the loaf and a thank you prayer is said for the bread of life; then a glass of wine is lifted and a prayer is said for the fruit of the vine.

* * *

Cantor Roth told her that it is up to the woman of the house to have a desire to make it a warm and loving home, create a clean and beautiful home to carry on a tradition for her family and guide these memories and traditions through generations to come. Thus, for every holiday that is celebrated, culinary dishes were created for the various holiday seasons of the year where the family prepares together and sits together and asks for thanks for whatever was given to them. Be it simple fare or more elaborate, the feeling of family continues through the generations.

For Maria, the lessons came easy to her as they were very similar to her home background. And she especially liked the unique dishes of the various holidays.

* * *

The first holiday Cantor Roth told her about was the New Year, which falls around the early fall and is called Rosh Hashanah, 10 days later comes Yom Kippur a day of fasting.

In the home, round Challas are baked, an act that symbolizes life without end—and a year in which there will be no interruption. The meal is begun with sweetness, like honey, so no bitterness comes in the New Year. The ram's horn (Shofar) is sounded in the synagogue to herald the dawn of another year.

* * *

The New Year's Dinner was basically the same as the Sabbath meal except for the addition of the honey and raisins and sweet pastries.

Today, we place cut apples on a platter along with small dishes of honey and we dip the apples in the honey for a sweet new year.

Raisins are added in the round Challas and are delicious for dessert.

* * *

Honey Cake

3 ½ cups sifted flour
½ cup strong coffee
1 ½ tsp. baking soda
½ cup vegetable oil
1 ½ tsp. baking powder
4 eggs
1 tsp. salt
½ tsp. cinnamon
1 cup strawberry jam
1 cup brown sugar
½ cup white raisins
½ cup shelled walnuts
½ cup honey
(½ cup dark honey -hold)
½ cup orange (or lemon) juice
zest of an orange (or lemon)

In a large mixing bowl mix all wet ingredients well, then slowly add all dry ingredients and mix well. (If batter is too thick, add ½ cup water.) Spray Bundt pan or large long loaf cake pan with vegetable oil. Pour mixture in the pan. Decorate the top with the ½ cup walnuts.

Bake in a 350 ° oven for 1 hour, test with toothpick to determine if done.

Allow to rest for 5 minutes. Turn out on platter and while still warm, drizzle all the remaining honey over the cake.

* * *

Carrot Tsimis
(Olga's recipe influenced by Maria)

1 lb. large pitted prunes
½ cup brown sugar
1 lb. dried apricots
5 large grated potatoes
2 lb. brisket
2 lg. chopped onions salt and pepper
3 lg. sliced carrots
Mom's spice
2 lg. cubed sweet potatoes broth as needed
(This recipe can be made vegetarian without the brisket.)

Prepare brisket:
Place brisket on a glass dish, season well on both sides and cool in refrigerator for one hour.

Sauté:
In heavy pan, add 2 tbsp. vegetable oil, and sauté 1 chopped onion, 1 sliced carrot, 2 stalks sliced celery.
Add brisket with all the juices; sauté on both sides; add ½ cup water; and dried fruits.

Simmer:
Cover and simmer for 1 and ½ hours.
While simmering brisket, sauté remaining onion in oil; add the grated potatoes. Set aside; season well and keep stirring until light golden.

Assembling and Baking Tsimis:

In a roasting casserole dish, place the brisket and juices; then layer the rest of ingredients. Sprinkle ½ cup brown sugar intermittently between the layers; add a little water or broth, cover, and place in a 350° oven for about an hour or more until meat and potatoes are done. Add broth if casserole is too dry.

This can be made the day before and refrigerated. The next day, slice the brisket across the grain, place on top of the potatoes, pour some gravy over the brisket, and bake for about 30 or 40 minutes till hot.

To Serve:

Place brisket on a large platter, surround with potato medley. Serve gravy on the side.

***

Yom Kippur

The Day of Atonement — A Fast Day

After the day is spent in the synagogues and temples asking God's forgiveness for our sins and not eating for 24 hours there comes the Breaking of the Fast.

All cold dairy dishes are placed on platters, such as all types of pickled fishes like salmon with cream sauce; pickled herrings with and without cream sauce; salted herring in oil; cold poached fishes in aspic; hard boiled eggs; chopped egg salads; cold borscht with sour cream; fruit compotes; coffee cakes; sponge cakes and honey cakes.

* * *

Hanukah

The Festival of Lights
Celebrated in December

After the battle fought with the Greek-Syrian occupiers, the Maccabees attempting to cleanse the Temple defiled by the enemy found only a small jar of oil, which miraculously lasted for eight days when lit in the candelabrum. The holiday commemorates that miracle and the little Jewish nation, which outlived its powerful enemies.

In the home, every night for eight nights, candles are lit in the Hanukah Menorah and gifts are exchanged. Children are given "gelt" (money) and songs are sung.

One of the traditional dishes served is:

Potato Latkes (Potato Pancakes)

2 cups raw grated potatoes
1 ½ tsp. salt
2 eggs, beaten
1 tbsp. grated onion
½ tsp. pepper
1 tsp. baking powder
1-2 tbsp. flour or matzo meal
¼ inch Canola oil.

Fry:
Drain potatoes; mix ingredients in a bowl. In a heavy skillet, drop potatoes by spoonfuls into hot oil; turn until golden brown on both sides; drain on paper. sprinkle a little salt on them while hot. If not serving right away, cover with foil and place in a 250° oven for a short while until ready to serve.

To Serve:
Serve with applesauce, whole cranberry sauce or sour cream and chives.

Purim Celebrated in the Spring

It is a joyous holiday. The children dress in costumes and grotesque masks, most of the boys dressed as the evil Haman and the little girls dressed as the beautiful Queen Esther who saved the Jewish people from his evil ways. Gifts are given to charity. A special triangular cake is shaped and baked, depicting the hat Haman wore, called:

* * *

Homentachen

1 pkg. dry yeast
1 tsp. salt
½ cup sugar
1 beaten egg
1 cup scalded milk, cooled off
1 tsp. lemon zest
1 ½ stick butter about 4 cups flour
¼ cup warm water

Mix and Knead Dough:
Place yeast in lukewarm water. Add a pinch of sugar.
Let bubble.
Cream butter, sugar and salt, add eggs, lemon zest, 1 ½ cups flour, milk and the soaked yeast. Work in enough flour to make a soft dough.
Knead until soft and elastic. Place in a greased bowl, cover, and allow to rise until double in bulk.

Roll and Cut Dough:
Roll out on floured board ¼ inch thick. Cut into 4 inch rounds, brush with melted butter and fill:

Fillings:
Poppy seed filling;
Prune or Apricot lekvar (jam);
Rasberry Jam with crushed walnuts, cinnamon and sugar.

Passover
(A month after Purim)

Passover, or Pesach, commemorates the deliverance of the Jewish people from Egyptian bondage, proclaiming that every man has a right to freedom.

The house has been cleaned; new dishes are used for this holiday and foods with leaven like yeasted breads and some grains are not allowed to be eaten for the next eight days.

The first two nights are the Seder dinner services conducted in the home. Family and friends try to come from far and near to re-enact in story and song the miracle of Israel's departure from Egypt.

Special foods are eaten during this time. The Paschal Lamb, roasted egg, the Matzo, Charoset (grated apples, nuts and honey, wine) and the bitter herbs. The wine in Elijah's cup is raised.

The youngest child is given the honor to recite the Four Questions:

"Why is this night different from all other nights?"

The usual Pesach meal is roast lamb or chicken, vegetables, roasted potatoes, and deserts of special cakes made without leavening using eggs and egg whites beaten into the cakes.

* * *

Shavuot
Festival of the Harvest The Birthday of the Torah

Shavuot is the traditional birthday of the Torah. The home is decorated with flowers and greens. Traditionally, dairy dishes are eaten in honor of the Law compared to the "land of milk and honey."

Cheese Blintzes (Crepes)

4 eggs
½ tsp. salt
½ tsp. sugar butter for frying
1 cup water
1 cup milk
1 1/2 cup flour

Mix Ingredients:
Pour pancake ingredients together and mix well with a whisk or electric beater. Cover and refrigerate 1 hour.

Fry in butter
Heat a small skillet, a black iron pan (crepe pan); lightly butter with pastry brush. Remove from pan and pour 2-2 ½ tbs. batter in hot pan, twirling pan to cover & spread batter on bottom.

Fry the thin pancake until golden and fry on other side lightly. Loosen edges with spatula and flip over on a large plate or cloth. Wipe pan with paper towel and begin anew.

Cheese Filling

¾ lb. cottage cheese
1-2 tbsp. sugar
1 egg pinch salt
4 oz. cream cheese
1 tsp. lemon or orange zest
1 tsp. butter
Mix all ingredients together, except butter.

Fill pancakes:

Fill and roll pancakes and place on a buttered sheet pan. Brush tops with melted butter. Bake in oven at 375° 20 to 30 minutes.

To Serve:
Serve with sour cream or fruit jam of your choice or fresh fruit.

* * *

Maria spent months learning and studying the culture of the Jewish people. She was very excited to surprise Nicolas with her conversion to his faith. She was immersed in the traditional bath, the Mikvah, and she cried with happiness. Tears came to Nicolas' eyes when he heard what she had done.

They went to Cantor Roth together and were married in the traditional Jewish way.

Chapter 9

The 1930s

*Maria and Nicolas in Havana Park in 1934
with their three children (from left) Olga,
the author; Ernie and Magda.*

Nicolas worked many long hours at the restaurant. By 1933, Maria had given birth to two daughters and one son. The political problems in Cuba continued, changes were beginning to occur in Europe and the stock market collapse in the United States, with the ensuing depression, affected tourism to the small island country. Protest resulting in economic crisis and in 1933, caused labor unrest.

Herr Otto sold his restaurant and told Nicolas he was going back to his country, Austria. The military, led by Fulgencio Batista, took over in 1933. The coup overthrew the liberal government of Gerardo Machado. As a child, Olga (the author) remembers standing near the window waiting for her father Nicolas to come home from the restaurant, and once saw him crawling in the street because of the bullets flying above him.

Nicolas made up his mind that he did not want to raise his family in such a corrupt country.

Nicolas' younger brother, Andrew, arrived in Cuba in the mid '30s and stayed with him for a few months and then left for America. Andrew had written to his parents and told them of the happy marriage Nicolas and Maria had, and that Nicolas was thinking of leaving Cuba.

Nicolas's parents wrote to him and asked him and his family to come and live with them in Hungary and to run the farm and the sunflower oil business for them. Nicolas thought about this long and hard and spoke to Maria about his parents' offer. She wanted this decision to come mainly from him and he wanted their decision to make her happy and comfortable with the idea. Finally, he made up his mind to pursue his original dream of going to America.

In 1936 Nicolas applied for a permit to enter the United States. While waiting, he sold the restaurant for less than it was worth. He left for the states and stayed with Andrew for a few months to establish residency until he received the necessary papers to re-enter with his family. It was very difficult for them to be parted. Maria remained in Havana with the children and Delia, who left the Farpons.

Finally, Nicolas went back to Havana for his family, and in May 1937, the entire family left for the United States of America.

They had passage to New York City on a ship leaving Havana harbor. How excited the children were! The two girls, Magda and Olga, were 8 and 7, and their brother Ernie was 4. Joseph and Aaron came to the harbor to see them off and presented the two sisters with two beautiful porcelain French dolls with authentic silk costumes. The dolls were left behind on the ship when they entered New York and there was no time to re-board to look for them. All of a sudden, they were not very happy little travelers. Their little brother held on tightly to the large metal toy airplane that had been given to him.

The passage took three days and two nights and seasickness overtook Maria and Magda so they stayed in the cabin most of the time. Nicolas took Olga and her little brother and walked the decks, went into the dining room and had delicious meals and they played with other children.

Finally, they arrived. As the ship entered New York City Harbor people were on the decks, most crying. Many have been waiting for this moment for so long. Nicolas and Maria held on to each other and their little family.

They had come so far, from their home country to a strange land with a new culture and a new language. The signs of upheaval and possible war were showing in Hungary and in Cuba, where they had found each other.

Now, they gazed upon the Land of Freedom where all their dreams and hopes for their future and their children lay. They closed their eyes and whispered a silent prayer, each in their own way.

Chapter 10

1937 to 1947

They lived in a small one-bedroom apartment in the Bronx. It was difficult for Nicolas to find a job. He found short-term ones in various restaurants and finally, he decided to do what he did best. He found a small candy store on the corner of Tiffany St. and 163 St. that was for sale. All he needed was a down payment of $300. Maria had put away some money before they left for the states. She gave Nicolas the $300 he needed. Nicolas was overwhelmed. The deal was finalized and in 1939, Nicolas and Maria were owners of a small candy store.

They moved to a small two-bedroom apartment above the store. They painted and cleaned the store. There was a small kitchen in the back, big enough for a stove and a sink and a worktable. There was a small walk-in cool room, which was used for groceries, fresh vegetables and a compressor for the soda fountain. A small icebox stood in the corner for the meat and dairy products.

They learned to make ice cream sodas and sell newspapers and candies. They figured out that if they could be open for dinners, they would bring in a little more income. A small menu was written and they began to serve dinner from 5:00 p.m. on. The dinner was a one-dish meal accompanied by Maria's home baked bread, for 65 cents. People began to hear about the delicious food, which was served at the Weiss' Luncheonette.

There were only 5 tables and there was a line every night for the dinner patrons. Nicolas and Maria's children went to school during the day, but they had to run home to help their parents at the luncheonette afterwards.

Maria began to bake her homemade strudels; coffee cakes, Danish and doughnuts filled with homemade apricot jam. They served the pastries with coffee all day. Their daughters served the pastries and they served the dinners to the patrons also. People would leave the girls 5 cents as a tip. The patrons loved her Coffee Dumpling Cake with Apricot Jam.

* * *

Apricot Jam

1 lb. dried apricots
¾ cup soaking water
1 ½ cups sugar
Wash and soak to cover apricots with cold water. Add ¾ cup soaking water, mix sugar well and cook until thickened, about 2-3 hours, stirring at times.

Place in jars and cover well. Refrigerate.

* * *

Coffee Dumpling Cake

1 envelope dry yeast
1 ½ sticks sweet butter
1 cup lukewarm milk
1 lb. flour

2 whole eggs and 2 yolks sugar cinnamon pinch of salt ground walnuts grated lemon zest

½ cup apricot jam

¼ cup vanilla sugar cake or cookie crumbs

Pre-heat oven to 375°

Prepare Batter:

Allow yeast to proof in ¼ cup of the warm milk; ½ tbsp. sugar and 3 tbsp. flour. Mix and let rest until bubbles form in mixing bowl.

Mix well remaining warm milk, eggs, salt, sugar, flour; and 1 tbsp. oil

Stir into starter bowl with yeast mixture.

Knead:

Add 4 tbsp. melted butter little by little while kneading dough well until it becomes shiny and separates easily from hand or beater.

Place dough in oiled bowl and allow to rise till double in bulk.

Roll and Cut Dough:

Sprinkle flour on a board. Roll dough till ½ inch thick.

Cut dough into rounds with 1-inch cookie cutter.

Prepare to Bake:

Butter Bundt cake pan; sprinkle with cake crumbs.

Dip dough rounds in melted butter and place on bottom of pan. Sprinkle with walnuts, sugar, cinnamon and lemon rind.

Place a second layer of dough rounds, dipped in butter, with ½ tsp. apricot jam in center of each round.

Alternate the layers, once walnuts-sugar-cinnamon and then, jam.

Fill the mold to the top. Cover top with melted butter and brushed egg.

Allow to rise about 1 hour.

Bake:
Bake about 50 minutes.
Turn out and place on a doily wrapped round platter.

To serve,
Break the rounds off with two forks or fingers and serve
on individual plates.

* * *

1942

The war affected the entire country. Goods were difficult
to obtain. Sugar and coffee was rationed. They sold the
luncheonette and Nicolas heard of a Cuban restaurant
opening up in Manhattan called "La Conga." They hired him
because he was able to speak Spanish and knew the restaurant
business. The owners, two brothers who were Italian Jews,
had come to America the year before. The restaurant did not
do well.

The following year, they decided to turn the restaurant into
a French nightclub called "La Martinique." They redecorated,
re-did the menu, hired a French chef and a large dance band
and presented entertainment.

Young new comedians and singers were hired who nobody
ever heard of. There was a different one every weekend.
Frank Sinatra, the famous Argentinian singer Dick Haymes,
Danny Thomas, Jackie Gleason, and Zero Mostel among
them. In the afternoon they would practice in the club in front
of the waiters. If the waiters clapped, they would continue,
and if not, they changed their material. Danny Thomas was
their favorite.

The first time Zero Mostel came to the nightclub, he was
ushered into his dressing room by Dario, the owner of the
club, and Nicolas. Zero placed his suitcase on a table, opened
it, removed a red tie, went to the closet and hung it up on a
hanger. Dario looked at the suitcase and screamed, "That's

your wardrobe?" Zero answered, "Yes, you don't like it? I'm leaving." It took both Dario and Nicolas to stop him from walking out. He was their only act that night.

Nicolas got close to Zero Mostel. He had come from a rabbinical home and they had a lot in common. Nicolas invited him to the house one evening on their day off. Zero took the subway with his agent to the Bronx and Maria served a delicious full-course dinner for him. He joked with the children and told Nicolas to open up his own place.

Dario heard about the dinner from Zero. He asked Nicolas if he were interested in being his partner in a small summer hotel in the Catskills and his brother, Alfred, would be his partner also and help him. Maria would do the cooking. Nicolas would manage the place and they didn't have to invest money.

* * *

Thus, the "Port Orange Mountainview House" in Sullivan County, New York was born.

The small hotel, with 25 rooms, was open for two summers. The entire family worked and the children helped out in the kitchen and dining room. There was a large apple orchard in the back of the property and a wide brook ran behind the entire length. The first year, Dario and Alfred wanted to cater to their newfound Hollywood crowd. Their prices were high and because the patrons mostly worked weekends, they would come in the middle of the week and rarely filled the rooms up.

For the second summer, six new family bungalows were added, a sun deck was built above the old barn, two tennis courts were built near the orchard and Nicolas insisted he wanted the hotel to cater to families. So they lowered their rates and they filled the place up.

Magda, their older daughter got married in the hotel that summer, in 1947. Nicolas sold his share to Alfred as he felt the entire burden of the business fell on him and Maria.

Chapter 11

Asbury Park, N.J.

*A postcard from Weiss's Hotel Altman, which Nicolas and Maria
ran from 1947 until the family sold it in the mid-1960s. The other
side of the card reads: Free Bathing, One Block From the Beach,
Dietary (kosher) Laws, Counselor-supervised Kiddieland.*

During the winter of 1947 the entire family moved to
New Jersey to a new business venture, Weiss' Hotel
Altman. They arrived in December. One of the fiercest
snowstorms ever was beginning to fall upon them. Maria was

not concerned about the storm. She knew her children would settle into their new surroundings in a small town and find new friends. Nicolas and Maria loved the shore-side hotel. They knew there was much work to be done especially before the buildings would be open for the spring season.

Olga was in her senior year in high school and received permission from the school administrator to do her last two semesters in one. Instead of graduating in June of 1948, she graduated in January of 1948. She would go to school from 8 to 4 Monday through Friday. No one from her family was able to attend her graduation due to business pressures. Her parent's partners came to pick her up and drove her to Asbury Park.

It was a very exciting time for all. Olga went to Asbury Park Business College to take secretarial and business courses. Her younger brother, Ernie, began his sophomore year in high school. The family was informed that their eldest daughter, Magda, would be giving birth the end of July to her first child.

For Nicolas and Maria, their lives continued with hard work in a large hotel business. It was a colonial style building, which was close to 75 years old then. There were two buildings connected to each other. The smaller building, the Annex, was open all year around. The family lived there. There was a small kitchen and adjacent to it, the "Tea Room" which had a dozen tables and chairs. This room was used to serve tea and fresh baked pastries to guests during the season and for a dining room for winter guests.

The main building held the lobby, main dining room and kitchens.

The first winter all 75 of the hotel's rooms were painted and refurbished. The large dining room, which sat up to 300 persons, was painted and re-decorated with mirrors on the several columns in the middle of the room and new drapes. The large lobby was painted and several new pieces of furniture were added.

It was very important for them to have a functional kitchen, which would be the heart of the new operation. Since it would be a Kosher-run business, there were two separate kitchens: one for meat and one for dairy. Two separate commercial dishwashers were installed also. There would be a separate pantry for salads, fruits and appetizers, and a bakery with a 4-tiered baker's oven, commercial mixer and large working table. Behind the bakery, there was a screened-in porch for cooling and storing the baker's trays. No one used the baker's name; he was always called Mr. Baker, even if he was different from one season to the next. Nicolas would make sure he hired an Austrian, a Hungarian or a German baker. Below this kitchen, there were large walk-in refrigeration rooms. The last one was a freezer. There was another large room downstairs with two bathtubs. The Koshering of the meats and fowl was done there.

Other rooms downstairs were used for storage: separate dishes for the Passover season, canned goods, and linens. There were four separate rooms to house the busboys and bellhops also. The female wait staff was housed on the top (4th) floor of the main building as well as the baker, second cook and pantry man.

The office was staffed by Nicolas and Maria's partner, Ethel. Her husband, Joseph, was a gambler and rarely there to help out. Olga helped Ethel with the typing, answering and booking the reservations and as hostess in the main dining room.

Olga had a ledger where she wrote the names of the guests, their table number and whether they had company for a particular meal. This information was then posted on their bill. She remembered everyone's names. The dining room was also opened to the public.

After the first two years, Nicolas borrowed money and bought out his partners. During this time, their older daughter Magda came back to the states with her two-year old son, and her husband. There was enough work for the entire family, especially in the spring, summer and fall months. There were weddings and Bar Mitzvahs also in the off-season.

In 1949, Olga met and fell in love with her soon to be life partner, Lenny. His family had a wholesale-retail poultry business. They married on October 28, 1951. Together, they helped manage the hotel.

Nicolas and Maria loved this business and made sure it was kept up well—painting every year and restoring the old structures. During this time, there was a large turn-of-the-century rooming house next door to the hotel called The Colonial, and they bought and restored this building also. They loved that house and planned to live there when they were older.

In the early 1950s a young man was hired to work in the dining room. His name was Sam, but was also called Alex. He came from England and Nicolas found out he was born in Czechoslovakia, had lost his family in the Holocaust, and he himself had been in a concentration camp. Nicolas saw something in the 19 year-old lad. He was smart and learned quickly. He was taught everything Nicolas knew about the restaurant business. Alex reminded Nicolas of himself when he first went to work for Herr Otto. Eventually, Alex called for his lovely fiancée Elsa, who was in England and had also lost her family during the war. She came and they were married.

After buying out the partners, finally, the buildings were ready for the grand opening. The kitchens were stocked with fresh kosher meats and fowl and fish; all kinds of produce and fruits; dairy items such as cheeses, butter, sour and sweet cream; pickled appetizers such as herrings, smoked and pickled salmons.

They went to New York City employment agencies and hired a second cook to help Maria; a breakfast and dairy cook, a baker and a pantry man. They hired eight waiters and busboys, dishwashers, chambermaids and two bell hops came from the local agency.

The opening was like a Broadway show. Olga ordered pink tablecloths and napkins and fresh flowers on the tables for the first Seder dinner. There were 300 people for the first meal and surprisingly most everyone was satisfied. The eight days of the Passover holiday continued with the kitchen serving three full-course meals every day. The tearoom was open in the afternoon and evening also where hot tea and delicious pastries were served.

The business continued, the family working hard to make it a success and Nicolas and Maria were at the heart of the entire operation. They always wanted their children to stay together and continue in the business, but it was not to be.

On May 1, 1960, Nicolas fell ill and died of a heart attack. Maria was beside herself. She missed him terribly, as did the entire family. She continued to work, but one could tell her heart was not in it.

In December 1965, Maria was diagnosed with a brain tumor. The surgery was in Mt. Sinai Hospital, in N.Y. Olga had a chance to sell the hotel property to a builder and Olga and Lenny and their children moved into a house in a nearby town. Maria came to live with her in their home and on June 8, 1966, Maria died.

Nicolas always had a smile on his face and was a very good-natured person and people loved him. Maria was a little more serious and very straightforward. They loved each other dearly.

After the hotel was sold, as a measure of her love for Nicolas and his faith, Maria donated the two Torahs that had graced the hotel's synagogue. One went to a synagogue in Asbury Park, N.J. and the other to Nicolas' brother-in-law's synagogue in Crown Heights, Brooklyn.

There are so many stories to tell about my parents. Perhaps I will write them down some time, but in the meantime,

I will write down some of the delicious recipes they had created together, not only for the hotel, but also for families and friends.

My parents have been gone for a long time. I like to think of them together in Heaven, drinking nectar from the Sunday Ladle.

Chapter 12

Chicken Dishes

Chicken Barcelona

3 peeled baking potatoes
1 large onion, sliced
½ red, green and yellow pepper sliced in strips
½ cup canola oil
1 large onion, sliced
3 diced garlic cloves
Entire chicken breast, cubed.
1 chopped ripe tomato
Paprika
Mom's spice to taste
2 tbsp. Tomato paste
Lime juice, Salt
Pepper Capers Stuffed olives

Sauté 3 peeled and sliced ¼" potatoes in vegetable oil until golden.

Sauté 1 large sliced onion until transparent in separate skillet.

Add chicken breast from a large roaster cut in cubes. Stir gently.

Add sliced red, green & yellow peppers, sliced julienne style.

Add 3 large cloves diced garlic and 1 chopped ripe tomato.

Add 1 tsp. sweet paprika, 1 tsp. Mom's spice, ½ tsp. each pepper & salt.

Add ½ cup tomato sauce, ½ cup broth, 2 full tbsp. tomato paste. Mix well.

Sprinkle 1 tbsp. capers, 2 tbsp. sliced stuffed olives, lime juice.

Mix, stir and simmer. Cover & cook gently until potatoes are done.

Serve on a large platter surrounded by ripe (yellow) Plantains with sliced lime on top.

* * *

Roast Chicken

With Potato Cocotte

Marinade:
1 4 ½ lb. roasting chicken
Salt
Pepper
Mashed garlic or garlic powder
1 lemon
Sweet paprika
Canola (or olive oil)
Wash & remove fat from chicken and place in a glass bowl.
Place all seasonings in a separate bowl with the oil and mix.

With your hands, rub seasonings all over the outside and inside of the chicken. Squeeze juice of 1 lemon on and in the chicken and place lemon skin inside cavity.

Wash hands with soap and water.

Cover chicken with plastic wrap and refrigerate for 2 hours.

Bake:
Place chicken in roasting pan with left over marinade and roast @ 350° for 2-2 ½ hours, turning every ½ hour, until drumsticks are flexible.

Place potatoes and small onions around chicken for 15 min in roaster.

Drain and place chicken on a serving platter. Top with sliced lemon and sprinkle with chopped parsley over all. Surround with potatoes and onions.

* * *

Potato Cocotte & Small White Onions

Red Bliss Potatoes, peeled
Small onions
With a melon baller, scoop out individual balls from peeled Red Bliss potatoes. Peel the transparent skin from the small white onions. Leave whole.

Sauté both in a skillet with canola oil and salt and pepper with a sprinkling of sugar till golden and onion almost caramelized.

Wait to place around roasting chicken for the last

15 minutes of roasting. Taste for flavor. Sprinkle with paprika.

* * *

Roasted Cornish Hen

2 Cornish Hens
Marinade
Salt
Pepper

Mashed garlic
Olive oil
1 cup orange juice
1 cup orange marmalade
Wash & clean chickens.
Place marinade (everything except marmalade) in glass bowl
Cover chickens with marinade and refrigerate 1 hour

Bake:
Roast chickens in 365°oven 1 to 1 ¼ hours, turning every 15 to 20 minutes.
Brush with orange marmalade each time they are turned. The Cornish Hens can also be made without the orange juice and marmalade and substitute melted Guava Jelly in the Marinade and brushed with the Guava Jelly during roasting.

Serve:
Serve on a platter of Romaine leaves surrounded with sliced citrus fruits. Alternatively, on plating, the chickens can be placed on a bed of rice (white or brown) surrounded with canned guava fruits.

* * *

Portuguese Chicken

1 whole chicken cut in eighths
1 large sliced onion
3 cloves garlic, diced
1 large can tomatoes
¼ cup olive oil
1 small can tomato sauce
1 to 1 ½ cup water
2 tbsp. tomato paste
1 lb. linguine

Basil
Small black olives
Fresh grated Pecorino Romano Cheese

Sauté:
Use a Wok or large heavy skillet Sauté chicken in olive oil both sides until color changes. Season with salt and pepper.
Remove and set aside. Sauté onions in drippings until transparent.
Add chopped garlic, the sautéed chicken, toss and mix

Boil:
Add tomatoes, tomato sauce, tomato paste and 1 cup water.
Bring to a boil. Break uncooked linguine in half and add to casserole.

Simmer:
Mix well. Lower heat to gentle simmer, mixing and
tasting for seasonings at times and cover. Add a few basil leaves.
Simmer gently about 30 minutes until chicken is done. Add water if sauce gets too dry.

Serve:
In a deep, large serving bowl, place all ingredients and sprinkle a small can of drained black olives on top. Sprinkle with olive oil.
Serve with Pecorino Romano Cheese if you wish.

* * *

Chicken Breast Wellington

Preheat oven to 350 degrees
Entire chicken breast with skin of a 5-6 lb. roaster
Lemon juice

½ lb. chicken livers, deveined, sautéed in olive oil with
3 oz. mushrooms
Vegetable oil
1/2 chopped shallot
Salt Pepper Butter
Pie crust or puff pastry from freezer section of market

Chicken:
Debone entire breast from a 5-6 lb. oven stuffer chicken
Wash well and place on a glass dish.
Sprinkle both sides with salt and pepper and juice of ½
lemon.
Cover inside of chicken breast with the liver-
mushroom pate.
Roll the breast and truss with butcher's cord. Season with
salt and pepper.
Sauté gently for 3-5 minutes on both sides in butter and oil.
Sprinkle with lemon pepper while still hot.
Place on a warm dish while preparing puff pastry or make
a pie crust.

Crust:
Remove pastry from freezer and unroll.
Arrange each sheet of pastry on a cloth, and brush
with butter.
Continue placing each sheet on top of each other until
there are 3 sheets all brushed with butter-oil mixture.
Place chicken in crust
Cut cord from chicken breast.
Place chicken breast on the pastry, and roll it until seam is
at the bottom.
Brush pastry with oil mixture.
Bake in a butter-oil casserole until pastry is golden brown.

Gravy

1 shallot, diced
3 oz. mushrooms, sliced
2 tbsp. flour
White wine

In the casserole where the chicken was prepared, add 1 diced shallot to the drippings, 3 oz. sliced mushrooms and sauté until mushrooms are done.

Add 2 tbsp. flour, mix well and using a whisk, add 2 splashes white wine.

Correct the seasonings. Bring to a boil to thicken gravy.

Serve:
Use a large round or square platter to serve and pour some of the mushroom gravy around the roast. Sprinkle with chopped fresh parsley Serve the rest of the gravy in a gravy boat. Sprinkle grape tomatoes for color.

Recommend:
Slice portions on a diagonal.
Couscous and asparagus would be a nice complement.

* * *

Chapter 13 Recipes

SOUPS

Vegetarian Mushroom Soup

1 large onion, chopped
1 large carrot, finely diced
1 long celery stalk, finely diced
Vegetable oil
⅛ cup and ⅛ cup salt
Pepper
1 - 2 tbsp. flour
tbsp. Mom's Spice
10 oz. mushrooms, chopped fine.
½ cup milk or cream (optional) Parsley, chopped
2 quarts chicken broth, low sodium

Sauté:
Sauté onion, carrot and celery and veg. oil till transparent with ⅛ cup oil
Add the mushrooms, mixing well at times until mushrooms darken.
Add rest of oil and mix.

Add the flour and seasoning, mix well one minute. Add a cup of cool broth, mix, then add rest of broth.

Bring to a boil, for one minute.

Simmer:
Simmer gently. If not thick enough make a slurry until soup thickens.

Add chopped parsley to soup. Correct seasonings.

Thicken:
Milk or cream can be added to soup when serving in each bowl.

Slurry ⅛ cup cold liquid, broth or milk add 1 full tbsp. flour

Mix well and add to soup, then bring to a boil each time until desired thickness is obtained.

Hungarian Bean Soup

(Vegetarian)

1 pound pkg. small white Navy beans (soaked overnight)
or 4, 14 oz. cans white navy beans
2 qts. chicken or vegetable soup, low sodium
1 lg. onion, chopped
3 cloves garlic, chopped
⅛ cup vegetable oil
Salt, Pepper Mom's Spice
1 tbsp. paprika
Spatzle
Dill
Combine and Simmer
Rinse beans and place in heavy soup pot.
Add 6 cups low sodium chicken or vegetable broth and
2 cups water.

Simmer about 1½ hours till beans are tender if using dry beans.

Sauté:
In a separate skillet, sauté 1 large chopped onion until transparent.

Add 1 chopped tomato, 3 chopped cloves of garlic and 1 tbsp. paprika.

Sauté well, then add everything to the simmering soup. Season with salt, pepper and Mom's spice.

Mix well and simmer gently while adding drop noodles (Spatzle)

You may puree the soup before the spatzle is added.

Spatzle

1 cup flour
Salt
Pepper
1 egg

Mix Together:
Mix well until a thick batter forms. If too thick, add a little water.

Hold a strainer with large holes over the simmering soup and pour the batter in the strainer. Mix with a wooden spoon and let the spatzle drip over the soup Mix the soup at times

Serve the soup in bowls with a sprinkle of dill and a dollop of yogurt or sour cream.

Country Tomato Soup

(Serve Hot or Cold)

1 28 oz. can whole peeled tomatoes, chopped
1 can tomato sauce

1 large onion, chopped
Basil leaves
1 tsp. minced garlic
1 can water
3 tbsp. olive oil
Salt
Pepper
1-2 tbsp. sugar

Sauté:
Sauté onion and garlic in olive oil.

Simmer
Add all the other ingredients and simmer gently for about ½ hour, stirring at times.

You may add chopped scallions, cucumbers, zucchini and/or a dollop of sour cream or cream or yogurt when serving. May be served hot or cold.

Oriental Corn Soup

1 14 oz. can creamed corn
1 tsp. cornstarch in 2 tsp. water
1 14 oz. can low sodium chicken broth
1 stalk chopped scallion
1 to 2 tbsp. Soy sauce
Simmer all the above and serve with fried noodles.

Butternut Squash Soup

1 Butternut squash, (cut in half and seeded)
1 large onion, chopped
1 large carrot, diced
1 large yam
1 stalk celery, diced

Salt
Pepper
Dash of nutmeg
Olive oil
1 24 oz. can low sodium vegetable or chicken broth

Microwave
Place squash on plate and microwave on high 4-5 minutes until soft
Place yam in microwave 4 to 5 minutes until soft. Allow both to cool.

Sauté and Simmer:
Meanwhile sauté vegetables in olive oil
Add the broth and bring to a simmer.
Scoop out the yam and squash into the soup pot.
Use a roto-masher or manual potato masher and puree contents.
Mix well. Correct seasonings and liquid for thickness. Serve in a bowl with a sprinkle of dill and a dollop of yogurt.
Note: You may use cream or if the broth is not thick enough, make a slurry.

Hungarian Potato Soup

2 tbsp. butter or olive oil
4 peeled and cubed potatoes
2 carrots
2 or more quarts water or broth
1 chopped onion
1 cup sour cream or yogurt
2 tbsp. white vinegar
1 chopped tomato
Chopped chives or parsley
½ green pepper, chopped
2 tbsp. flour

Salt
Pepper
Paprika

Sauté:
Sauté in 2 tbsp. butter or 2 tbsp. oil, 2 carrots, finely chopped, 1 chopped onion, 1 chopped tomato and ½ green pepper, chopped. Add salt and pepper. Sauté until onions are translucent. Then add 2 tbsp. flour. Mix well.

Add cubed potatoes and 1 tsp. paprika

Simmer:
Pour into mix 2 quarts water, or more to cover.
Simmer, covered until potatoes are done
With a potato masher, mash some of the potatoes while in the pot.

To Serve:
Place 1 cup of sour cream in a soup-serving bowl.
Pour some of the soup on the sour cream and whisk well.
Finish pouring the rest of the soup in, whisking well. Sprinkle with chives or parsley.

* * *

If you enjoyed Olga Weiss Hipschman's family story and cookbook, check out the other cookbooks we have in our catalog, as well as other titles you may enjoy from BluewaterPress LLC at http://www.bluewaterpress.com.